Gumption pervades Erin Keane's fab new collection, *Death-Defying Acts,* the whirligig world of circus folk lit up by the poet's verve. But fabrefaction alone is never enough: Keane helps us see the aerialist's ambition as our own, how "So many ways to fly" characterizes the carnie and the midway we call our daily lives. And here, we thought we weren't freaks.

—Alan Michael Parker

What does the tattooed lady fear? "Some day I'll run out of skin." What does the reader of *Death-Defying Acts* fear? "Soon, I'll run out of poems in this wonderful book to read." Even coulrophobes and circus haters (that's almost everybody in the twenty first century, right?) are going to be drawn into these weird, precise, grimly funny monologues by clowns, freaks, the aerialist, the lady lion tamer, and her lion (yes, the lion gets some of the best lines in the book). Erin Keane's characters are living on the existential edge, as we all are, but they know it and we don't, usually, except at 4 a.m. on the way back from the bathroom. If you always wanted to run away to join the circus, avoid this book. If you always wanted to live near the scary edge, peering over into the abyss, read this book. You'll wish it were longer.

—Richard Cecil's most recent collection
of poems is *Twenty First Century Blues*

Erin Keane's circus is filled with beautiful losers. The tattooed lady, clown, lion tamer, aerialist, Zorada the fortuneteller, and even the lion speak eloquently of life on the outside but inside the heart of a weird art. Who among us has not felt the beast's breath on our neck or seen our bodies covered with stories. These pages tell us what we felt and how we still feel in the dark before sleep.

—Barbara Hamby, author of *All-Night Lingo Tango* and *Babel*

Death-Defying Acts

Death-Defying Acts

POEMS

ERIN KEANE

WordFarm

SEATTLE, WASHINGTON

WordFarm
2816 East Spring Street
Seattle, WA 98122
www.wordfarm.net
info@wordfarm.net

Cover Image:
Cover Design: Andrew Craft

USA ISBN-13: 978-1-60226-005-4
USA ISBN-10: 1-60226-005-2
Printed in the United States of America
First Edition: 2010

Library of Congress Cataloging-in-Publication Data

Keane, Erin.
Death-defying acts : poems / Erin Keane. -- 1st ed.
    p. cm.
ISBN-13: 978-1-60226-005-4 (pbk.)
ISBN-10: 1-60226-005-2 (pbk.)
I. Title.
PS3611.E16D43 2010
811'.6--dc22

                                                                    2009045138

P 10 9 8 7 6 5 4 3 2 1
Y 16 15 14 13 12 11 10

for Drew

Contents

Maybe at last, being but a broken man,
I must be satisfied with my heart, although
Winter and summer till old age began
My circus animals were all on show,
Those stilted boys, that burnished chariot,
Lion and woman and the Lord knows what.

—WILLIAM BUTLER YEATS, "The Circus Animals' Desertion"

Jesus, send some good women to save all your clowns.

—BRUCE SPRINGSTEEN, "Wild Billy's Circus Story"

The Corsican Brothers Circus Presents: Death-Defying Acts!

In Montserrat County, kudzu adorns
telephone wires like stockings
in the bath of a black and white movie.
We slink in around midnight, following
the advance man's arrows that point
our way to your grounds. It wouldn't matter
if you came to spend your week's mad
money or stayed home playing euchre
and catch—our crew still blooms a tent
out of whiskeygrass by daybreak. Midway
concessions scream to life. Our miniature
small town joining yours for a tight hand
of nights in late July when your kids
tire of chlorinated days and want nothing
more than a game of chance, a sugar
tornado, the exquisite horror of a sideshow
ticket burning a palm. The Dairy Dell
will not compare. And you jovial farmers,
you redfaced salesmen, Junior League ladies
and bored local belles, you will come to us.
You will wind your way up state highway
arteries into our pulsing lot, you will
clutch your handbags and hard-won prizes,
count ice cream stains in the carousel
glow. Hand on her knee, you will ascend
out-of-body in a Ferris wheel car, seeing
none of our faces from that fleeting height.
What will you take from our battered trailers,
patchwork tent, three rings thrilled with delight
and fear?
   You have come for one reason,
and it is time. Step into our heart and cheer.

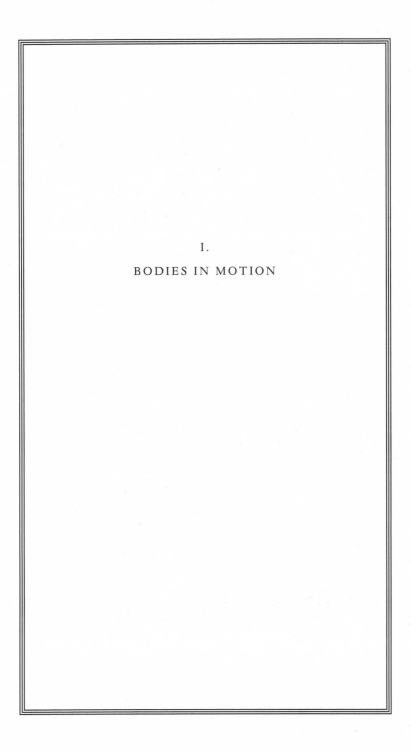

I.

BODIES IN MOTION

Two Cannibals Are Eating a Clown— One Turns to the Other and Asks, "Does This Taste Funny to You?!"

If the groundhog can face
his shadow without a freak-out,
giving us an early spring, surely
I can go out bare-faced,
unashamed. Right—
and the bearded lady could just
shave!

A sick joke, moving
Clown Alley by the sideshow,
though we're all human
oddities to the lot lice crawling
the grounds. Still, a soapy cloth,
some water, and my balloon-inked

cheeks run red: I could almost pass
for a person, blending into townie crowds,
while the Human Worm inches along,
begging Milly Pinhead for a light.
There's value in deformity—

freaks flex in plexiglass stalls, a peek
is all you need, while I pile
into a Volkswagen with twenty
more clowns, shucking and gagging
for a laugh. Underneath the wig,
the clothes, behind my thick paint,
no damaged DNA marks me mutant
but I'm on the show, made-up, playing

the audience—the wacky dances
and honking rubber noses,
the ten thousand jokes I've told
and retold until they're all I hear
every time I roll to a new show,
                            wondering
if anyone can see the monster
twitching under my skin,
                    dying not to get out.

Lectio Divina of the Tattooed Lady

When you wake up, brash morning
busting through my gauzy curtains,
gloriole outlining this rollercoaster
of a body, use one finger. Trace
the green, blue, black, violet ink

carved into my skin, words from wounds
healed to beautiful scar. This is how
I mend: epidermis knits, but raised,
a topographical map, a kind of Braille.
Read me slow, mouth into the pillow—

bawdy apocrypha circling ears, down
to symbol-studded ankles, antiquity
transformed under Airstream roof
and you might as well learn something
after such a guilty night. Alphabets

intermingle. *What are you trying
to cover?* you ask, anonymous
novitiate, until I shush your mouth, drag
palm over apologia—*je ne viens pas
ce soir vaincre ton corps*—running

down my back. A small lie, blessed
but you linger, discerning what
I will give. Lay your thinking
aside. Runes etched behind my knee
reveal: it hurt, sure, but *only the one*

who inflicts the pain can take it away
frames my shoulder blade. Rest in me,

listen. Take what you will. I know:
it's all surface, it's all that keeps you
from cutting me open to count the rings.

The Lion Tamer's Act

Until you feel on your neck a dank breath
and the hint of teeth, like a new girl's
acrylic nails, how can you know blood
rushing out through artery, in by vein?
I have learned to read a jawline:

scan for tension—too loose, he loses
focus, yawns, smacking chops. Tight
means a trap snapped shut—
the bone crush! O the girly shrieks.
I dwell in the space between.

Trained for cues, he poses still. Cup
his muzzle, spread the jaws. Nobody
told me: how I would fall into blank,
dull eyes, my lungs flattened, useless.
There's one way in and two ways out.

When I'm in there, my mind goes
pliable, a fabric softener sheet, balled
up, then unfurled. His mouth, my head:
act natural. Count back, ten to one—
spectacle feeds on illusions of control.

The Aerialist Grounds Herself

Edge of the earth, slippered toes balance,
flexing. A platform lip, a spotlight. Freeze.

Unfrozen, instinct tips reflex: the inching
climb backwards. Stepping down, rung after rung.

Ring of mine, your perfect circle has no end, no
beginning. Rolling steps in reverse, sawdust swirling.

Swirl of ten thousand faces, a blur. Shocked
murmurs roll over me, out the door, music swelling.

Swollen hands begat swollen hands, arms without
question. One man's door is another man's window.

Windowless, a tent seizes air and holds. There is in
and there is out, but only within. All questions catch.

Caught in empty space, tumbling weightless, within,
a window is a door. Is a trap. Is a trapeze. Is a ledge.

A Tamed Lion's Dilemma

Amusing enough, our games:
treat for trick, what I won't do

for a touseled mane, a rump
steak cube. My paws press her

girly shoulders, horns grunt
our leonine waltz. My breath so

sharp on her neck. The algebra
of appetite—so much depends

on x. My cage, her ring. My
tongue lolling: she smells like syrup

& smoke. Some kinds of love
have you both on your knees:

her head inside my mouth agape.
This tension, hard to beat—

the hunger, the snack, they taste
the same: a little salty, a bit sweet.

Pretty Young Girl and a Handsome Lad: A Strip of Four Black & White Snapshots from the Midway Photomat Booth

I.

In the booth, every inch
is a yard. Three fingers
could fit between them
with room to spare. She
twists a finger through
her hair, chews on one
nail. Eyes rough denim.
He makes a silly face:
happiest fish in the sea.

II.

She is giving it her all,
teeth bared straight
at the lens. *Write this*,
her eyes throw back
at us. He's a farmboy
with a prize calf: so
eager, trying to press
temple to temple, but
O her getaway blur.

III.

How he got hold of her
hand, we'll never know.
He's raised it to his lips,
plants one large on her
third knuckle. Bold boy.
Shock, dread: those old
twins tapdance her face,
dragging what looks like
a future behind them.

IV.

A rope of muscle, his
arm coils her. Porcelain
teeth reflect the flash,
so cocky. Her mouth
half-open in mid-word:
what she's saying goes
without saying. Curtain
flapping, he will be left to
wait out the developing.

The Tattooed Lady's First

At fifteen I believed I moved in a rarified
bubble, all feeling in the world contained
within, the dichotomy of *in* and *out* sharp,
a line in the crackling dust of a dark
television screen: me *vs.* all. That summer,

I grazed on fudgesicles in the shadow
of an abandoned power station, dragonflies
zipping in tandem through skeletal metal:
tumbling trapeze act, wings beating
a rivergreen trance. Mating in thick
August air, they hovered my sticky hand,

the clacking of Walkman cassette reels
unnoticed. I played one song ten thousand
times, my theme, headphones keeping it
private, between my ears—an illusion
of singularity, of experience. They flew off,

skimming a stagnant puddle, the fallow
transformer dull under dwindling light,
not humming. I didn't have words
for the pins and needles. A mosquito

lit down and sipped from my thigh.
I fingered the welt, blood drops
smearing my leg. The red against white,
almost membrane, almost a wing.

I knew a place. A guy with forearms
graffitti'd like boxcars. *Somewhere*
they won't see, I whispered. All you
have is your skin, and what it covers.

How Do You Get a Clown to Stop Smiling? Hit Him in the Face with an Axe!

I'm not trying to be a nightmare, but please
yourself—*coulrophobia*, this kid's mommy
says, covering his eyes, as if,
under my name in the yearbook, ran my greatest
ambition: *to scare the shit*
out of little kids! Lemme tell you what's scarier
than clowns:

               death, for starters, worse
than that, dying alone—pissing yourself,
coughing blood, last breaths labored in
and out, wondering when the Meals on Wheels
gal is gonna stop by with a hot lunch to find
you, maybe a week later, when your
                            Labrador

finally gives it up and starts eating your leg.
That is something to wake up nights
over, crying in the dark, huddled under
a Star Wars blanket. Afraid of clowns, what the fuck
kind of phobia is that?
                    We're neutered trick
poodles in greasepaint, not a 747,
or a skyscraper roof, see: I don't even use
bugs, or snakes, or rats in my act, so what's
the big deal?
               When you've seen a pretty girl's
eyes go blank after risking *hello*, talk to me then,
son, tell me if a day's worth of beard under white
still gives you the terrors, if a guy in floppy shoes
can equal a biopsy, your wife's lawyer,
                         your father
after a fifth of Wild Turkey, look me straight

in my made-up eyes after seven sleepless
   nights in an empty bed
and tell me the irrational is still more
frightening than walking out
your front door every morning,
that looking me in the face is so much worse
than anything your twisted
little mind can imagine, that you've been so
fucking lucky that
                      I'm
enough to give you the shakes.

The Tattooed Lady Falls

What blooms from the end
of a needle? Numbness: a way
to stop time during my afternoon
rotation, the dry tented air trapped
in bubble-wrap, swaddling my near-

naked form. There are fast ways
to forget the crawling eyes, but I
have a better addiction: another
needle floods a bouquet of exploding

Touch-Me-Not twisting my arm,
punishing: skin is not an open
invitation, though I love to be
watched. I could cruise into edge-
of-town honkytonks, but one
late-August knife scarred La Sirena
of my forearm, learning my lesson.
I've only been looking for a sure-

mouthed man: for that I might swallow
the largest sword. Today, I caught the hungry
eye of a clown in the dusty setup—
sweaty roustabouts humping tent pegs,

bolting the tilt-a-whirl into the ground.
We stood still in the moldering shade
of the elephant truck, dew squishing
my toes. *You're built like a violin,*
he told me, leaning close. My snare
drum heart tapped a rapid, rhythmic
beat, echoing violent, even in retreat.

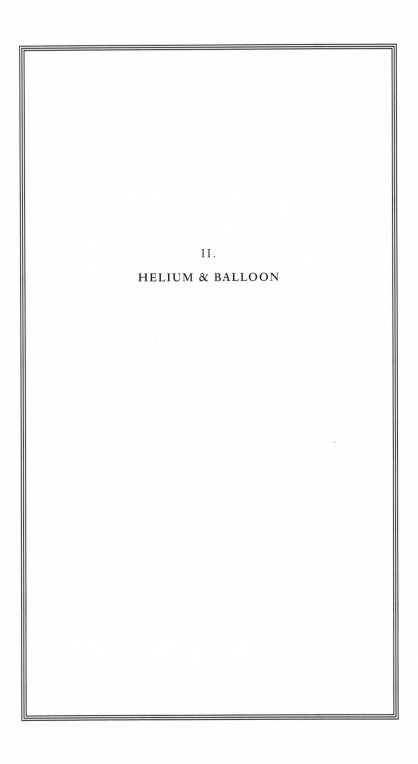

II.

HELIUM & BALLOON

Joe Buck Yourself!

When I fell into this gig
I fancied myself a true harlequin,
reviving commedia dell'arte
one county fairground at a time
but the clownmaster took
one look at my diamond-pattern
tunic and declared: *say, Jack,*
you'll fit in the fringe just fine!

So goodbye, Arlecchino,
                          hello
Howdy Doody drag—
I learned the lasso, harassed
the ringmaster and roped
his hat, studied *Midnight Cowboy*
for Jon Voight's walk, mimicked
his guns-a-blazin' pose with
                          air horns
but found myself rewinding night
after night for Enrico Salvatore
Rizzo: feverish, nervous, profane,
his lame little leg dragging
behind like a busted suitcase
full of borrowed hats, cheap
suede, a needlesharp need.

Why do cowgirls walk
                          bowlegged?
'Cause cowboys eat
with their hats on!

Clowns never
score. I tweaked the corny costume,
ditched the bandana and ten-gallon,
made the character my own.
Ratso the Clown: cigarette
dangling from painted lips,
I got a quick mouth and faster
fingers—left hand plucks
a quarter from behind your ear,
the right slips in your pocket, comes
out with a wallet, burning a hole.

The Lion Tamer's Visit

Tiny marquee lights pulse, firefly
glow casting the door. Something
pulls me to the freak tent, to snake
charmers and the Dog-Faced Girl.
Face burning, I admit: I want to watch.

The sawdust smells different, more
human without the menagerie.
Johnno the Geek poses Christ-like,
sword slow-dipping his throat:
arms outstretched. Hilt gleaming.

Stalls and stalls in even rows. Fire-
eaters flashing, the Armless Wonder's
finger-toes grip a bow, fiddling old
mountain songs. I hide in back. On
a platform: Miranda, the Tattooed Lady.

Rotating positions, she's living statue—
first, painted David, one coy arm
curled up, then shoulders twisted,
our Venus de Milo full-fleshed,
unapologetic arms in flaming bloom.

Pose of the Tattooed Lady

Here's where I feel like a whore
with a heart of gold, arched vixen
in a silver bikini, your fist of dollars
buying a ticket to exotica. I know
how to play the light, make your dry
tongue search for comfort, or dream:

will I step my high heels down
from the platform and into your lap,
add your name in red to my infinite
sleeve of heart? Will I make you forget
your father's never-tender hand? Hardly,

you're a mark, but you believe
me human—it's only when you
cup your date's hand I feel my gut
rebel, I see my role in a mythology
out of control: I, too, watch and
yearn. I count my blessings. What

will you take from me? Your eyes
burn twin holes into my sternum,
so I twirl, a jewel-box ballerina.
Are we frozen cryogenic here,
the audience and the art? Or will I
grow old with you, tempting eternal?
All fiction, both helium and balloon?

Zorada Consults Her Magic Ball

Ask Zorada: *what will I be?* Better
not tell you now. Ask again later. *Will*
I be pretty? Outlook good. *Will I be*
rich? Outlook not so good. *What will I try?*
Reply hazy. Try again. *Should I paint*
pictures? Very doubtful. *Should I sing songs?*
Most likely. Or: decidedly so, you
may rely on it. *What lies ahead?* Can't
predict. Concentrate, ask again. *Will we*
have rainbows day after day? Sources say
no. Don't count on it. Or: as I see it,
yes—definitely! It is certain. *So,*
what will be, will be? Without a doubt! All
signs point to yes, but: my reply is no.

The Aerialist's Signature Stunt

What I know can fit in the palm of a hand. Energy: potential,
kinetic, chemical—mine. Fly bar released, I throw the trick.

Tricky things, those hanging traps. My high swing, his
easy catch: ankle, Andrei's hand. Release me back.

Back-tracking the air, I twist, my angled momentum. Feet
catching ledge, again released. *Talia, my dragonfly, my bird.*

My burning ears. His chalky palm-lines ghosting: heart
and fate twist glitter tights. Father's mustache smiling.

Smile tight, do not let on. With every catch, the next
trick: a body in motion tends to stay so. Keep moving.

Moved to pause, I might fall into waiting hands, rigid,
an object: a pocketwatch pendulum, seconds tocking.

Ticking breaths, I throw my bar: catch, hold, ponder a fall.
Potential, my gravity. How they weigh so heavy in the palm.

The Tattooed Lady's Visit

I have the eye of a crow. Light reflects,
and I want. What can I trade for the gleam
in your eye? It is enough to live to be
seen, enough to be stripped of all
symbols. How young are you? I am
older than I admit. Caught with more

books than most clowns dare, I
fingernail the spines smirking against
the shelves. *Poets*, you say, *mostly
foreign: Yeats, Mayakovsky*, needling
the slick side of a record—something

French. Grooves in the album show
what will come next. Each play, a diamond
tip rubs the surface, wearing vinyl down.
On the wall, a photograph: three towheads,
three small t-shirts and sunlight squints
facing the camera from the frontline
of a summer day. A woman, head thrown

back—faint, tight, brandished smile.
My mother, you murmur, suddenly
behind me, *a professor*. I lie and say I'm
an orphan, your face so close to my ear.
My father is dead, too—your breath
a wriggling fish on my neck. Three

sets of frayed canvas shoes on boys
in the photo. Something about the crook
of the middle one's arm, fingers clutching
his hair. My hips forgive the obvious

music, relentless needle: your mouth
hungry on my shoulder. Brass buckle
embossing the small of my back.

The Lion Tamer's Résumé

At least in this gig, you wear a gun,
pressing your thigh like a trained
Great Dane ready to snap. A needlesharp mind's an asset, memory is gift—
recognize the mouth twitch and know:

to crush or caress, this means another night
on the road. A trade to teach a daughter,
unlike my rank years on the girl show,
grinding, scissoring legs. *Work strong,*
the bally urged, barking my wiggles.

County-wide farmers stared. One girl's
work is another girl's past. *No ladies,
no babies*—just me, whiskey-soaked,
hand-made tassels twirling *Girls! Girls!
Girls!* Big tent's green light taunting.

I play the night over and over: *get out—
no daughter of mine* echoing, uncovering
behind a trailer for the boss. *No tits, but
you'll do.* A gun. A whip. *Are you in
or out?* I stuck my finger in his mouth.

Clown in Full Makeup and a Woman Tattooed: A Strip of Four Black & White Snapshots from the Midway Photomat Booth

I.

Dark bangs frame her
face: she barely reaches
his nose, at least twice
broken. Two profiles.
He's tilted her up to him,
his fingers fit the inked
outlines on her chin. Lips
parted just enough to
say *we are still breathing.*

II.

Now they are arrows,
a two-way street. She's
glancing down and past
him, lilies exploding her
cheek. Eyes lit, he is
an ecstatic saint, palms
receiving the stigmata:
a bit reluctant, his pale
face turned up to God.

III.

The next frame could be
blank, but white heat is
its own reward. Flash
has backfired, shining
too bright a light on
our pair. The burn and
the dodge: what lingers
dark around the edge,
like ink or running paint.

IV.

His hand clutching her
hair, exposing a world
map on her nape: so
bold in the foreground.
Black wings feather her
shoulders. The back of
her head. He's curved
in, mouth on her neck,
trying to pass for tender.

The Lion Tamer's Letter

My fingers in the cat's mouth, I think
of you and me sleeking cobblestones,
backs flat on alley-brick walls. My father
echoed curfew, your elbow crooked
my cheek: a geometry of promise.

How I counted breaths until the bells
of St. Augustine clanged midnight.
You smiled, every day yours to own.
Crackling, static electric, we jumped
fire-twirled hoops: in, out, through.

I see me, posing ancient marble, stars
tangled in your hair. I couldn't tame
my tongue—arching out of town,
chronic mouth cursing. I write, never
call. I've yet to lick the stamp.

We won't get caught, but the road
or the curio cabinet, it's always
a choice. There were two ways out—
me gone, shamed. Or married,
pulsing luminous: fireflies in a jar.

I Ask Her to Tattoo a Single Tear on My Cheek

What's done is done, forever. I rewind the night,
from charred dust to whoosh: our tent aflame,
a supernova. They all burned up. I have no right

to be alive. Reporters, cops I told ten thousand times
how I slept, sick—I'm bad news now, my lasting shame.
What's done can't be undone. I see them still at night:

that boy, his shirt, his hair, a roman candle sky;
the moon from over my left shoulder, ashy gray.
A supernova spent, my luck cashed left and right.

I woke, ran out, when horns blew "Stars and Stripes
Forever," code for *something's wrong*. My feet of clay.
What's done is never done. I froze that night—

a core collapse, a neutron star, and my baptismal names:
lone witness, exile, clown undone. What never came.
What's done is never done. My curse, my sleepless nights:
exploding supernova, burning heart that can't beat right.

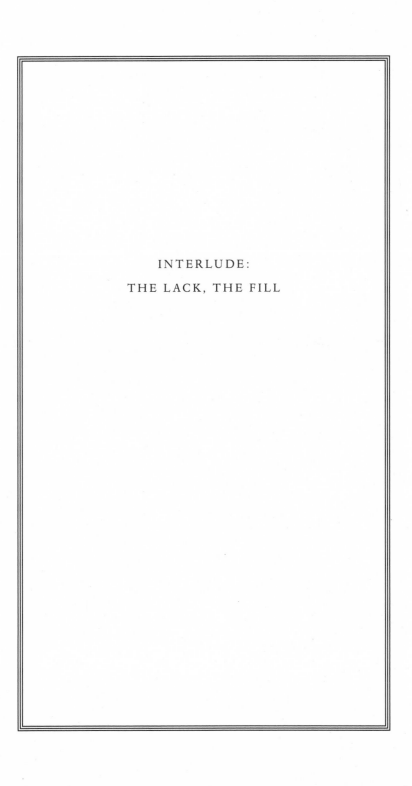

INTERLUDE:

THE LACK, THE FILL

Claude Waits for Miranda

Passionflower vines tangle the timbered frame of a ramshackle
shop's front porch, luring bees and hummingbirds already so
early in the season, and when he leans temple to crushed velvet
curtain, he sees: dragon-green lassoing her ankle, snaking up the
calf's crowded portraits, spreading from canvas of thigh to cracked
leather seat then running down floor, sweeping in all directions
and up the walls until a whole room smothers under pendulous
incarnata blooms.

A purple corona, five-stamen'd stigmata: remembering her first shy
peel of cotton, the two-inch insect he rendered in the pink high
above her farmer-tan, all bottle-glass lace and the faintest sheen.
How she returns in the coolest early morning when the sun still
shies along the baseboards, and he touches up the faded glimmer
of a wing first, before taking her next order.

He can tell time by her visits, after and before the lumbering
winter, wondering what tiny offering she will command, what he
can add to her, and sure as the spice drifts in from a cracked, gilt-
lettered window, it will be soon.

Claude waits, his needle hand twitching. The vines, stirred by an
unexpected breeze, do appear to be breathing.

The Lion Tamer's Interstate

Cross-country blooms apologetic
and I know my only stillness outside
a black hole mouth. Sneakers sway
optimistic from telephone wires.
Billboards rise, a swelling chorus.

Our season moves forever west.
I ride with the crew, leaving my cats
the cage. I have earned this, only—hours
of wheat, of feed corn pulsing my lids
in the deep dawn of burnt-sienna fields.

America's breadbasket kaleidoscopes
to life by the green-yellow glow
of the dash. Coffee bitters my tongue.
All afternoon, I'll sleep, your town
animated, a waterballoon dream.

The soft questions liquid in, then
out. Last night's girl under my arm,
neck fur-soft in the sun. Today, under
the radio philosopher's mossy purr,
we will know all there is to know.

The Aerialist Dreams of Walking

Around midnight, things take place—another creekbed,
another graveyard. Imagine: secret planet, starfish hand.

Hand-me-down skybed, heavens promise far-flung
fortune: dancing cheek-to-cheek, other face shadowed.

Shadows jump—strange heavenly, floodwall dancing—
how monstrous he could be, how dazzling of tooth.

Teeth and the lips stretch such a smile that jumping
in is relief. Me against the volcano, dew-point rising.

Raise me from soaked grass: heaven is mine and relief,
I am beyond relief. Smooth, featureless, his face molds.

Meld me to the moon tonight—wet fog hangs silver,
breathless: rodeo bareback, my grass-stained find.

Found out, I would face a gulf, a wide-open face:
by the creek, graveyard—it's midnight, I'm here.

If It's Not One Thing, It's Your Father

After the digging, my brother
Tommy leads us in prayer. We three
hold hands, chant the only prayer
we know: *St. Anthony, St. Anthony,*
 something is lost
that needs to be found, like we're
kids again, wandering the lot
with Mom, straining to be first
to spot the parked car.
                                          His voice
squeaks on the fourth round.
I choke my laugh down.
Mumbling benediction, I tilt my face
to the ground. Twenty years
overdue, the headstone: *Francis*

staring like they say he would
when called by his
full name—same bottomless
eyes as my baby brother,
a slight man squeezing
my fingers.
                      It was Aunt Kate
who decided that funerals
halfway across the country
were no place for kids, turning
off the TV set to tell us.

Tom's voice trails off, Frankie's
feet sink into the dirt, soft
from the sprinklers. Remember

Mom crying into the phone
on a Sunday.
             Nothing but dust
in the box and the rare fragment,
ghost face at the end of a glass.

We were sent for
to bring him home, to fill
   the gap
in the family plot, to fix
what has always been broken.
Our myths:
             the Dread Pirate,
the Viking chief, Conquistador
off on a mission.
                    Somewhere.
Playacting his funeral, it was nothing

like this grassy park, leaves coughing
in the wind. How did they launch
his Valhalla flameship
into the sea?
             There was a lot
we didn't know.

No kids between us, but
thousands of miles.
My brothers chased him down
every gin-soaked alley,
tightening our mother's
lips: *just like your father*. I became

a fool, eager to absorb
             the blows—
hitting the road, finally, seeking

a theme in vain.
                    Duty done,
I head back to the show, my
inheritance—his cap, green tweed—
pulled low: a mockery of a man
in the sharp noon sun.

The Tattooed Lady Transforms

Slipping the leather seat, skin
squeaks, I sigh—my Claude
drags his pen and I settle in
for a long session, the needle
humming, stinging, so many
cleansing bees. His palm on
my back, a communion, inking
chains into gills. A tadpole,

sloshing this amniotic parlor:
me swaddled in southern
gothic vocals, crumbling fiddle
made electric. How the pain
clarifies: it is a choice, a thing

made, created and re-created
to right. Claude tells his own first:
a wolf, and how he ran beers
for bikers until they gave him
a job. I picture him a lost boy,
so soft, his face clownwhite

then vanishing. Heat radiating,
morphing me aquatic, finger-
tips elongate to fins: feeling
my way the ocean, a juvenile,
full of promise. So many ways

to say *hallelujah*: the deep ache
of skin to be touched, the descant
of redemptive cover-ups, gasping
grace in empty spaces, the lack
only needles and ink can fill.

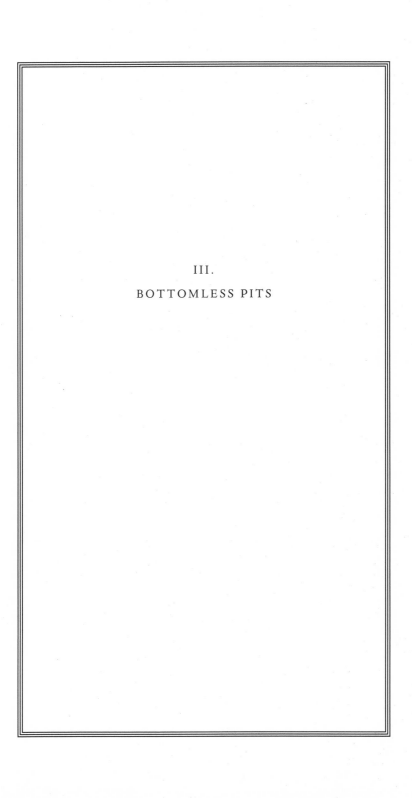

III.

BOTTOMLESS PITS

The Aerialist Puts on Her Shoes

I could fly before I walked. Tumbled head over
knee, sloshing the womb, waking mother.

Great-grandmother's hoops twirled Moscow,
brought Ringmaster down, tender knee begging.

Beg for ground, a different tension. How to be less
ornamental. There is up and there is down, forever.

Every tense night, a chance. Buttons escaping dilated
eyes, fingers bar-numb, I fumble. Awake, barely.

Bare feet catch better than slippers, but satin shines
in spotlight. I button them, under and over. Soft stepping.

Stop me from sleepwalking tightrope. Light blooms
the window, midway shine. Taut tendons pulling.

Pull the door: from in to out, easy, like waking.
I could tumble, sleepless. Or I could walk, not fly.

A Clown in Trousers

I got no grandfatherly gentleness,
it's true—so what can I offer
a kid like you? Truth?
Well, truth laid bare
can be a kind of kindness,
the sort of thing in short
supply around here.
                        So kid,
think hard about what coats you:
is it the chrome of a trailer hitch
being tailed? Are you the fishing lure

at the end of the mind? Or a sand grain
layered in crystalline
                        oyster spit?

And what will you do with the softness
inside? You're a wild, bored girl—
you'd end up here sooner
or later. What I do
could undo everything.
The truth is we're both
the worst kind
                        of frivolity,
useless as cotton candy, yet
here we are after the spotlight
dims, your first taste
of bourbon, my only visitor
in days. So you're here

to learn things, but I only
know this: you will never
go wrong hearing David Bowie

in your head
any time you walk into a room
alone. Now you tell me

something—what does
flying feel like?
                    How does your hand
feel when you reach
for the bar? Does the air
in your palm carry
weight, like a phantom
object? And how do you learn
to breathe while you tumble?
Sometimes I, too, feel my
me is too small—

what's the difference
between a circus and a
chorus line? A circus is
a cunning array of
                    stunts!

I know, you came here looking
and all I got is booze and jokes
and books and old albums.
But this is it, kid:

we don't know how to let
the universe rest.
                    Life should
take you somewhere. It might
be too late for me, but for you,
there's all the truth you need
in the violin,
                    in the crude, lovely drum.

The Aerialist Answers

Inching high wire, I triple somersaulted, my death-
defying act. Arms tucked under, then spread.

Spreading the canvas ceiling, a blush—vertical
axis defiance. A body at rest. They pulled me up.

Up and over and under and down, a body in motion:
infinity plus one, but gravity and the net stop me.

My hand feels this when I reach for the bar: my tether,
well-worn. No release of the *I,* only audience eyes.

Eyelids flutter on landing. So many ways to fly: to know
the tightrope's heaven, the looking-glass siren call.

Calling my name, father snapped fingers. Trapeze
in the air: flying ankles grabbing, sequin back-flash.

Flashes—a door to walk through, a window to look in—
do not diminish. Tucking fingers under arms, I inch away.

A Woman Battled: A Strip of Four Black & White Snapshots from the Midway Photomat Booth

I.

Three scars sweep up
her face: finger trails
in wet sand, hangovers
from shooting stars.
Her whiskered cheek
turned to the lens, she
aims one unflinching
eye, radiating a pair
of tiny, creased lines.

II.

Once she was lovely,
though now it's more
like the arched grace
in a cocked eyebrow,
a sinewy arm curled
behind her head, deep
corona: a mane in this
light, alluring like a
jellyfish, certain to sting.

III.

These booths being
what they are, shadows
creep in, framing her.
Over her head, two
dark points hover like
ears. Below them, her
pupils pop, courtesy
of the flash, fireworks
twinning her eyes.

IV.

She roars her head up,
prominent teeth bared,
moved by a music we
can't hear. *I have killed*
for less, her chin says,
face slightly blurred,
both mouse and cat:
play and fear circling,
that tarantella dance.

The Aerialist Remembers

Burn it: hissing, twirling glass, finger over palm.
Wolf teeth in slanting sun. *Princess! Fancy Tights!*

Tightening, fingers grip smooth handle. My palm
tilting, sunning locust to flame. Mother echoes.

Echo, Mother calls me, *she loves her voice*. Says *don't
talk to sideshow kids*. Cheeks burning, I promise.

Promises are nothing until broken—slipping one way
in, another way out. Whispering, burning in corners.

Cornered, a lion roars, whip-flash lightning. Thunder
rolls the tent. We tremble: whispers, unseen.

Seeing's in my blood—she flips my wrist up, nails
like needles. Trembling, I whip back my hand.

Handing needle, she taunts. *Do it,* eyes rolling. *Do
it?* I echo. Injured bug flutters. *Kill it,* she hisses.

Zorada Reads the Aerialist

Sooner or later, she always comes back,
yes? What is it this time, huh, Papa's picked
another handsome boy? Life's tough, princess—
tend your own garden, blah, blah: you want
my eyes? We let the cards decide. I deal,
you turn. The king of swords sits in judgment,
your page of wands a shiny coin. And O
you upside-down star—wheel of fortune spins,
but hanged man's always watching. I can see
your future, princess: turn a five, balance
gone, and then—I'll never tell. Must be rough,
this ace of cups you can't touch. Think the moon's
to blame? Smart money's on older loves: fool
and death, hand in hand, whispering your name.

The Lion Tamer Writes Another Letter

All that I know I am teaching this girl,
little beauty like I once was: remember
when you stole me from the cotillion, hell-
bent for Bogalusa? It was all I could do
to collect my white gloves from the floor.

All the Aunties gasped *Céline!* waking
my parents from sitting sleep—like that,
she wants the whip, my boots, she wants
to climb inside the cat's mouth and sleep,
wants to pull out his claws, one by one.

I'll teach you: I gave in, guiding her
shoulder, slight as a sparrow. Right foot
in, left elbow out. How to move the cat.
How not to get caught: the lion, the guy,
it's the same story, all the same snap shut.

Fighting the floor, she twitches *en pointe*,
flexing her instep, swallowed mid-spring
as if she's just learned about gravity, as
if a strong wind could scatter her, a spent
dandelion, through the rough sawdust ring.

The Tattooed Lady Watches

The problem with me is my memory
is bad, rotten like forgotten pears, so
I slink into ink shops for permanent records,
a life rendered in skin. It's vanity, sure,

but it's also a living. To recall is to know
half the story—I am a wide-open
book. The problem with you is your
look-don't-touch: Braille's just bumps
until it's read, and one man's gospel
is another man's rag, so which am I

tonight? I watch you burning, oil-lamped
and trembling all night in your trailer,
marking a card deck, nursing highballs.
Pulling cigarettes from your ear,
you think you're alone with your naked
face. You're only bold in costume,

but what you have can be undone.
What you don't have could fill
at least a back, maybe twirl up over
a shoulder, coy clavicle snake, spilling
across a chest. *What do you look like*

underneath? I asked, thumb-smudging
your paint, but you pushed me away. I
could trace your palm on my shoulder,
broken outline, but an earlier version
of the same story is already there. Instead,
I echo you, first with paperclips, then
with needles, in and out, pricking.

A Clown Without Pity

Listen up—when a liberty
horse stomps my foot
because I flicked a
                cigarette
in the wrong direction,
                  my screams
are not for your
amusement. Even the show
has room for real hurt—
it's a pissed-off half-ton brute
and on his back rides
a showgirl who can't
save me. Sure, I know

my place—a fool's just
a funhouse mirror: your
grotesque twin, slaughtered
ten thousand ways to bust
your guts, to make you feel lucky,
like you could never,
                ever be me:
sad sack, butt of the joke,
unbeautiful klutz, an effigy—

I only die once, but for such
   a long-ass time!

So when your kid whines
at the end of the show, don't
tug my sleeve. I got no more
balloon giraffes tonight.
Don't clown me to make
your girlfriend think

you're a bigger man. I am
a grown man in makeup
   for you:
my feet too big, my car
too small, and all the heroes fly
through the air—yet here
I am with a pie in my face,
a fat foot, and Quasimodo's
limp/drag. We fools know:

no matter how many times
you fail, you all get up
and give it another go, though
the seltzer bottle's always
   rigged,
the whoopee cushion always
lurks. We are tiny things,

downed like shots, and even
pratfalls bruise—so don't
laugh so hard, asshole: who
else could I be but you?

Zorada Reads the Clown

Your hand speaks for you. No luck. No love
but that which comes harshly, resisted—you
drop a pebble in a lake, it ripples lines
back onto your palm. I can read. Look how
your hand trembles in mine, see the outline
of a life. Ovals on heart line mean battle,
but yours, the long road: a romantic! Shall I
show you the girl? Tell me I'm right—you
have few lines but an old soul, she wears life
on her chest. You think your sorrow mound
fatter than hers, your suffering grand, but
you're wrong—you want what can be invented,
she will take what comes. What to do? Come
see me when you lose something. I can find.

The Tattooed Lady's Fear

Some day I'll run out of skin, the last
patch wasted on lotería icons or tiny
scraps of Edith Piaf lyric—some
fancy. I could keep an inch square
for the ultimate ink, the etching
at the end of the mind, but naked

spots burn like a bare bulb, so I
rush to cover what winks through
my dimmed bedside lamp. The little
pricks of pain comfort: I can
still wince, still feel at the end
of a shift in the tent of the living

wonders. Imagine my project
finished, the last tableau touched
up to perfect, final flourishes curling
around the Last Supper enjoyed
on my back, Latin prayers running
through seams left between life
after death and sideshow scenes.

Will I turn, then, to other surfaces,
tagging floodwalls, shaking aerosol
to free the paint, palming a marker
inside my frayed pocket? The perfect
and most flawed outlaw, my eyes
outlined in permanent mask? Or will I

roll inward, all scissors and paste,
magazine remnants collaging the panels
of my trailer? And what comes when
I have no story to tell—not even a fill

for that free spot in a two-dimensional
frame? No flaming mouth, hydrangea
eyes, your relentless, wormy hair?
My fellow bottomless pit, I see you
branding me across games of chance,
darting the chests of unmarked girls.

IV.

LIVE GRENADES

Clown in Full Makeup and a Pretty Young Girl: A Strip of Four Black & White Snapshots from the Midway Photomat Booth

I.

Loose waves waterfall her
face, a little Veronica Lake.
Birdy shoulder turned in
toward him: a black shirt,
painted mouth twisted.
Her eyes adrenalined, lip
sucked in. His face tilted
down, fingers tangled
in his shock of dark hair.

II.

She has made him sit up,
look the camera in the eye.
This is one way to have
a life. He is trying not to
smile. Arm around him,
she laughs, she is sunrise
on the first of May, new,
and he: in this second, no
longer a burnt-out match.

III.

Her mouth hovering his
ear. Maybe it's a secret.
Maybe her hand's on his
leg, but what's cut off, we
can't see. Fourteen years
between them shrink. He
looks off to the right, out
of frame, jaw soft. Thinks:
a separate moral universe.

IV.

Now his mouth, though
painted to turn down,
grins like a Labrador,
his eyes shut to reveal
diamonds. Her head tilt
says: *much better.* Blood
fills her cheeks and his.
O evidence, evidence:
her white-frosted lips.

The Tattooed Lady's Prayer

Take the Angelus swelling my
lower back, turn *spiritu sancto*
into tangles of coral, kelp
reaching full fathom five
from the sea. All the men,
cover their names in tribal
black ink swirls but yours:
my pen, my tongue, O salt
of my salt. He slams me

down like tequila shots and
I'm the quicksand hole? All
the apostles say *bullshit:* give
Simon's eyes a jaded roll. To
the curve between finger and
thumb, add this line: *Lord,*
to be thirty-three forever. Ignore

my scars. You know how I get
when I'm nervous. You know
my dime-sized heart on fire,

the one like the medal I wear
on my neck? Around it, fashion
a wooden block, a blank face
exploding from the cranked-
open top. On that punch box,
etch his name: *The Greatest*
Show on Earth.
                     And the heart?
Char the edges. Keep the flames.

Joke in a Box

There's nothing so lucky as Jack
   springing
from a painted trap with the crank
of a wrist, so early Friday
morning. In the punch box, then
   out then
in your calligraphed hand—I wake,
I think, to a simpler, homespun
time—O, but
             presto!
I'm a weedy joke-in-the-pulpit,
tangling handbills from my
last show and me lost
in the singed corners, always.

Call me: bog onion,
brown dragon! Call me
   tomorrow?
Here's what my roots
can do: I'll swell your tongue,
slur my words, burn your
weepy eyes, and still
you'll take me home.
               Call me
a bad penny. Wait for it, hold

your breath. Jacks coil
into themselves, protecting
a tentative inside, such delicate parts,
O, the *ha ha* on you. And will you
turn up
       a half-laugh, at least,

when what can only be
the first flower of spring
   explodes
your 3 a.m. walk? I am everything
and the misfortune—
I have done what must be known
   as my best.
I've tucked four-leaf clovers
between my toes, scanned
highway shoulders for coppers
   landed on heads—
I've pointed the elephant's trunk
sun-ward and braided his hairs
into lucky rings, counted
ten thousand ladybugs spitting
over their shoulders, knocking
on wood
               to keep the death away

and still I am nothing
more than the sum
of my charms.

               Let's break all
our legs—will I crack the embered
curse I drag behind me, so many
Leonid showers sprinkling dust
in my wake? Will you forgive me,
then, the start I can't finish,
   the checks
my mouth wrote? I am sure they
will not cash—
               here we go 'round
the merry-go-round, here we go
and come, and how do you find

me? Do I not know?
                          This is the way
I watch it flame, watch them burn,
this is the way we touch and go: here
I go again, all the old apologies,
    a tail-end
in the snake's ever-hungry mouth.

The Lion Tamer Demonstrates

Illusion feeds spectacle, the only thing
we control—audience *O!*, a well-timed
flourish, crack of my whip. Untouchable,
I jump him through hoops, rewarding
with meat. He's not doing it for me:

you test a cat's comfort, then you
invade. Move into the outer circle,
he retreats, into his inner ring, he'll
charge—onto the stool, I back off, he
stays! Teetering in the space between.

Teach him to sense your focus, train
your eye on every deadly muscle:
feel his sheathed claws twitching
your chest, even while you sleep—
dream the cat, a bed of tail and teeth.

You want to know about danger,
adrenaline jangling—you can't force
a cat to perform. Each time we step
into the ring, the lion and I know: we
dance for each other. I hold the gun.

The Aerialist Tries Her Hand

Blade-keen, I can slice a tent in two: wagon wheel,
little cannonball—knees up, head down, grenade pinned.

Pinwheeling, my heart a drugstore volcano, I test
the cage, skeleton key rattling—a stilted girl: unsure.

Surely the tamer knows. She nods, yellow eyes
steady. A cage for one, a door: I reach, my move.

Moving cat to ring, her commands echo: in, then out.
Lion's eyes flash, brass buttons. Soft roar my way.

My wayward clown unicycles, orange flash trailing—
focus. Smooth ivory handle fast in hand. First flick bites.

Biting down, I control pain: first cracked hands, now a leg
boasts pistil of red: raised kiss on skin already bruised.

Bruises bloom indigo, ripen to peach. Whip-slicing
the air, I crackle: borrowed boots, a live grenade.

Ascension of the Tattooed Lady

One morning you look up at last
night and realize you have been
on this show for too long, you've
packed your story into crows' feet
grooves pinstriped with shooting
flames. There should be another

way to have a life: no more 3 a.m.
wasted walks, knuckling *love*
and *hate* through the headlights
of passing trucks, no more *Dear
John* flash above your hem, hips
childless after all they've seen, holy
dove and hand grenade faithful
alike. Ingénues don't know until

they become the femmes fatale:
how to write a year on the tip
of a toe, how to taste more
than sugar when you lick,
why you throw salt over a
shoulder so it lands on luck.
Sins go nowhere: they rest on

the surface, flat as maps, rivers
running thin like the faith
of a muse. I'm ready to bust
gravity open, to rise up through
a tissue-paper sky—cracking
surface, your last glimpse of me:
my shining soles, rubbed clean.

A Fool in Four Letters

It takes lots of practice
to fall on your ass
                    like this—
I should become
a mime, my mouth
will be the death
of me yet: cartoon bubbles
poof forth, machine-
gunning clouds I attempt

to stuff back in but
they escape, floating
toward you, trailing
                    I'm sorry, I'm sorry...
which is a lie, you know—
pretty girls are to be kissed
and I am no kind of a man
for it.
          Yeah, clowns are
funny people: only
160 women went down on
    the Titanic
but all they wanted was a guy
with a sense of humor!

    What's 18 inches long,
    purple, and makes
    women scream?

Forget it, I got no punchlines
left, only questions and every answer
leads me to this:

       absolution
makes the fool grow harder,
even small forgivings
                shrink me back
to every coach and priest and cop who ever said
  you'll never be a man, Jack!
I can shovel all the
            whatever
you have into me and
it will never be
         enough,
it will be ash through my fingers—

and still the chagrin, still one more
game of chicken with a
               parked train,
my chronic red eyeball staring
  down the barrel
of today's irresistible, flaming fiasco.

The Aerialist Pays a Visit

I am a catch, the trap. The bar, a cage. Is a cat. Is a
key. Release. Magnetic feet pull, O different world.

World of mine, so sleepy—how odd. All the soft
questions. Pulling up window, I tumble out.

Outside, our show snores midnight rumble. Brides
rest tight in beds, no question. Father echoes: *married*.

Marry Andrei, how. To be less tangible, slip of a girl.
Cracked hands trail the cage. Lion rumbles gentle.

Gently, cage pulls hand, pulls key. To slip inside,
to spread his jaws, crawl head into mouth on fire.

Fiery cheeks, a baptism, a name: *Talia, crushed*. My
Jack blamed, my burden. Shame. Tumble the lock.

Lock to key. A trap, my feet. This world no different
from the rest. Blame me: the cage, the cat, the release.

The Lion Tamer Wakes Up

Sleep a blown dandelion, I bolt
upright, my bunk a bed of claws:
I can feel a wildness let loose
from the bars, tendon spring
from cage to floor, so easy.

What I can see: the cat slinking
darkened midway down, on
the hunt—or worse, past tents
to nearby farms: daughters on
needlepoint pillows, foaling barns.

Pupils grow wide, adjust to low
light. Maybe a shadow, maybe
a tail wrapping the corner, hinting
at what waits behind: hungry
muscles purring, a jaw untamed.

My crouch, my crawl, my low
approach: a cat from afar, a trunk
up close. Still second—a throaty
rumble, sawdust crunch: his dank
breath. The back of my neck.

The Tattooed Lady Takes Off

Someone woke the passed-out band,
blurting "Stars and Stripes Forever"
with boozy urgency and finally,
that's my cue: I'm done with this
disaster. For each town, I have a plan:

a way to be permanent, a roadside
attraction. Slipping through broken
voices, the chaos rushing, I hit
the ashy road. When morning breaks
over Aphrodite's Mermaid Show,
I'll flash silver in a string bikini:
a tossed grenade, daring the big boss
to send me home. Climbing into

the tank velvet, the water will sting
my eyes, my hair a fountain pen leak,
prayers blurring into every story
I wish I never told—torch songs,
an underwater piano heavy-tangling
like barbed wire: you familiar sign,
you bluebird of regret. Knives in ivy
will still twist my neck. No demi-plié
while latex-bound, my feet will flip
the fin. O siren surfacing. What good

could come from my mouth? Nothing
but the familiar gape of men eager
for that old pillowbook, miracle
and mystery—an authoritative desire,
what you wanted but could not take,
what you searched for in the waning
interstate light: an indelible trace.

At rest in the fishtail Bolshoi, my storied
skin will peel, shed,

then ripen to scales.

Where Will They Find Another Man of My Caliber?!

For my next act, I will soap
my face, strap on a helmet,
and climb into the heart
of a cannon—relax! It's no more
dangerous than shaving
                    with a chainsaw:

two hundred pounds
per square inch of compressed air
will propel me, parabolic
confessor, at seven times
the force of gravity—*our old
nemesis!*—and what will 65 miles
per hour teach me if not too much

tension, I'll sail over the net,
twirling through candycoated air
over heads cocked in perfect,
gaping wonder, or
                  too loose
and I'll miss my mark,

sliding, stunned—
                  listen! Once,
brown pelicans left the coast
and flew into the desert,
famine-starved, seduced
by an airfield's layers—
pregnant heat, aloe cool—mixed
by reflected sun, a miraging

tarmac shimmering deep
into a lake: an invitation to dip,
to fill their broad beaks with
   gravel
instead of fish, but
                roadrashing,
they skid across the blacktop—

you can't be shot straight,
to keep your neck, you've
got to tumble in mid-
air, landing in the net
on your feet, but what I want

is the blackout, the part
where my brain goes flat
in mid-flight, when
   everything slows
to a lo-fi crawl, I want one

way out: over and over,
every night the tight iron
sleeve, the sonic
           boom—
and the up and over and under
and down into the filament
web waiting, finally, the blue
silence on the other side:
           a body, my god, at rest.

Acknowledgements

Humble thanks to the editors of the following publications in which these poems first appeared:

Minnetonka Review: "Lectio Divina of the Tattooed Lady," "The Tattooed Lady Falls," "The Tattooed Lady Transforms," "The Tattooed Lady Watches" and "The Tattooed Lady's Fear"; *Nimrod:* "Joke in a Box"; *Phoebe:* "The Aerialist Pays a Visit"; *Open 24 Hours:* "A Tamed Lion's Dilemma"; *Bloodlines,* an anthology of emerging Kentucky writers: "The Tattooed Lady's First" and "The Lion Tamer's Résumé."

I'd like to give special thanks to my editor, Marci Rae Johnson, and to Andrew Craft, Sally Sampson Craft, Dickens, and everyone at WordFarm; to Richard Cecil, Barbara Hamby, and Alan Michael Parker for their kind words and support; to Troy Alvey, Emma Aprile, Zach Bramel, Nickole Brown, Martha Greenwald, Pamela Steele, and Terri Whitehouse for nurturing these characters and their poems; to Josh Strader at Big Brain Productions in Omaha; to Kevin Prufer and the Poetry Factory; to the She-Poets workshop; to Colleen Abel and Tom Doran; to the Kimmel Harding Nelson Center for the Arts and the Kentucky Arts Council for money and time; to my amazing community of writers in Louisville and at Spalding University; and to my families, both given and chosen.

Notes

The quotations in "Lectio Divina of the Tattooed Lady" are from "Angoisse" by Stéphane Mallarmé and "Erotica" by Madonna.

"Zorada Consults Her Magic Ball" is composed of answers from the Magic 8 Ball toy and lines from "Que Sera Sera," written by Jay Livingston and Ray Evans.

"A Clown in Trousers" borrows liberally from the Peter Bogdanoff translation of Vladimir Mayakovsky's "A Cloud in Trousers."

"Clown in Full Makeup and a Pretty Young Girl: A Strip of Four Black & White Snapshots from the Midway Photomat Booth" borrows a line from Top Stoppard's play *Night and Day*.

"The Tattooed Lady's Prayer" is indebted to William Shakespeare's *The Tempest* and The Hold Steady's "Stevie Nix."

"Ascension of the Tattooed Lady" was inspired by Hans Memling's triptych, "The Resurrection, with the Martyrdom of St. Sebastian and the Ascension."

Acknowledgement also goes to the following sources, which provided me with invaluable insight into circus life and lore: *My Turn Next: the Autobiography of an Animal Trainer* by Roman Proske; *Freaks & Fire: The Underground Reinvention of Circus* by J. Dee Hill; *Carnival Strippers* by Susan Meiselas; *The Circus: Lure and Legend* edited by Mildred Sandison Fenner and Wolcott Fenner; numerous accounts of the 1944 Hartford Circus Fire; Circus Flora in St. Louis; and the movies *Wings of Desire* and *The Greatest Show on Earth*. I also borrowed many tasteless clown and circus jokes, origins unknown.